WHAT PEOPLE ARE SAYING ABOUT GUY CLAPPERTON:

"Speaking effectively to the press is an important part of my role, Guy led me through a realistic and challenging process that provided a really useful framework that I can repeatedly use to properly prepare myself for interviews and media communications more broadly."

— John Coulthard, Microsoft

"Guy Clapperton media trained three of us and by the time he left we had a better idea of how to market ourselves to the press and formulate our PR messages. He also helped us hone our skills sets when working with journalists."

— Louise Dunne, Managing Director, Auriga Consulting

"We hired Guy as a media trainer on two separate occasions. The participants of the sessions were varied - from several different departments and with varying levels of previous media experience and training. Guy was able to both prepare our spokespeople for what to expect of a media interview as well as provide advice and expertise on how to speak to and interact with journalists, to make sure that they get what they want of an engagement, whilst we also accurately communicated our brand and message. In addition, he gave thorough background on the media and working lives of journalists, which gave context and really made sure that all participants truly understood the way that they work. I wouldn't hesitate to recommend Guy or hire him again if future training was required."

— Nicola Frazer-Reid, Marketing Manager, Mindjet UK

"We invited Guy to run media training for our senior executives in early 2013. Guy is hugely knowledgeable on the priorities and eccentricities of the media. He has powerful insight into the emerging world of social media and explains what we all need to know with clarity and without recourse to jargon. We particularly enjoyed the role-play element of his course, and we went away feeling confident and well prepared."

— Richard Leyland,
Head of Marketing Communications, Bango

"Guy was an inspiration for our small team. He was able to build upon the skills of seasoned PRs and develop the confidence of a new account executive. We still refer back to our media training with Guy and it certainly improved our results with the national newspapers. Not only is our telephone pitching better, but we revised our whole approach following our session. I would definitely recommend Guy to other PRs."

— Kate Warwick, Managing Director, PR Savvy

"Different clients need different types of training. Guy has adapted his training to several briefs and has worked closely with me to identify and acheive clients' individual objectives. We've had every kind of spokesperson to train from outright timid to outright public liability - and every shade in between. Each and every time they've walked out of the room a whole lot more able and confident than when they walked in."

— Claire Thompson, Managing Director, Waves PR

"Guy's media training for the Alcatel-Lucent team in Belgium was excellent. The team were delighted with his knowledge and especially his ability to bring the best out of each trainee placed in an interview situation. As Paul Spruyt commented: "Guy really knows his stuff. Great day, thanks!""

— Lucy Handley, Department 83

SUNMAKERS

Guy Clapperton

HACKED ABOUT

How to make press interviews and presentations productive for business

HACKED ABOUT

How to make press interviews and presentations productive for business

Published by Sunmakers, a division of Eldamar Ltd,
157 Oxford Road, Cowley, Oxford, OX4 2ES, UK
www.sunmakers.co.uk
Tel +44(0)1865 779944

First Edition

Designed by Ayd Instone, www.sunmakers.co.uk

ISBN: 978-1-908693-12-9

Guy Clapperton

www.clapperton.co.uk

To Carol for putting up with all this pontificating for all these years – and to Microsoft's public relations department for calling up and asking whether I did media training in 2002. I checked the bank account and found out that yes, I probably did, and only while they're reading this will they realize they were the first…

Acknowledgements

It's tricky to know who to acknowledge in a book like this. Every media training session I've ever done has contributed to the blog that made this book happen; however, a great many clients prefer to remain anonymous. The ones who comprise my 'worst media training candidates ever' certainly won't thank me for naming them (but thanks guys, you really need to read this although I suspect you won't). Every media training candidate, every interviewee in my journalistic life, has a stake in this book.

A number of public relations people have been very good to me in putting media training work my way over the years, some more than others but without their referrals the work would have dried up long ago. In 11 years I've enjoyed almost every session, and in that 11 years I've had too many to list individually so I'll offer a blanket thanks to them all.

John Lettice and Bobby Pickering gave me my first full time job in the press. Thank you. Their successors who led me to suspect I'd be better off freelance in 1993 I won't embarrass by naming (mind you, they were right). The editors who've kept me in commissions since then from the Guardian and elsewhere have been brilliant.

In terms of the sections on presentation I need to thank Mike Quinn from Adobe who got me involved in speaking to a greater extent than I'd been before, Alan Stevens who persuaded me to join the Professional Speaking Association and becoming a Fellow and Jeremy Nicholas who is another fellow media trainer and speaker, and a considerable support.

Any references to attempts at stand-up comedy you might find are down to Tim Dingle, whose courses I can recommend to anyone who doesn't mind finding a new skill and getting completely hooked for their mid-life crisis.

Finally if you think this looks like a professionally designed book then it's because Ayd Instone designed it like the professional he is. Had I stuck with the DIY approach, you'd know about it.

"I think it well to remember that, when writing for the newspapers, we are writing for an elderly lady in Hastings who has two cats of which she is passionately fond. Unless our stuff can successfully compete for her interest with those cats, it is no good."

– Wilmott Lewis

CONTENTS

Introduction

Hi. Thanks for buying or downloading this blook. My objective in writing it is simple and it's the same as my mission statement while I'm media training. Many people find press interviews or just standing up in front of people and speaking stressful and unproductive. This shouldn't happen but it does. This blook and my courses to go with it will allow you to be different. It's as simple as that. We'll look at your objectives and how to achieve them, common errors, good practice and how to make your press engagements and presentations sing. That is why I wrote this blook.

Blook? Is that a typo in the first full sentence and many times afterwards? From a senior journalist, or indeed old git? Many people will be wondering about that but it's not. 'Blook' is a word coined from 'Blog' and 'Book'. It's been around for just over half a decade as far as I can make out. Most of the thoughts in here are edited from my blog at Clapperton.co.uk – for updates, more recent thoughts and stuff I've found since, feel free to dip in anytime. This is a collection of entries from late 2012 to mid-2013.

This affects the structure of the book of course and hopefully this will work in your favour as the reader. I wrote the blog to be digested in very quick bursts, make a good point and get out – so you should be able to dip in anywhere and find something useful. Of course you can read from beginning to end if you wish but it's really a collection of thoughts and pointers put into some sort of order by collecting under subject headings. There isn't an over-arching narrative or theme – just (I hope) some helpful stuff.

I hope you find the insights, based on 25 years of journalism and over 10 years as a professional speaker, useful and that as a result the hacks don't do you over – or indeed, that you don't get hacked about.

Guy Clapperton
London, June 2013

Section 1:

Dealing with the press

TAX

wages

RATE RISE

usiness

tax

Shares dive despite profit boost

profits

trade

Mighty

tax

Mistakes people make whilst dealing with the press

I've been a jobbing journalist since 1989, initially in the trade press and then freelancing for the Nationals, broadcasting a bit, writing books, speaking a lot. Sometimes people make mistakes when engaging with journalists - here are some top mistakes people make:

We don't work for you: And yet many people in PR and marketing still call up and tell us exactly what they want us to write, where they want it in the publication and complain when we don't parrot their marketing messages. It's inappropriate; we absolutely owe you accuracy, but we're not part of your marketing arm and can't be treated as such. (By the same token you don't work for us, and if we tell you we need a quote by a given time and you can't help, that's just tough).

Independent doesn't mean 'on your behalf': If I had the proverbial penny for every time someone has told me they want a piece written independently and then told me who to quote and said I mustn't be critical of their client, I would have a proverbial fortune. If you want something in marketing-speak, you probably don't want an independent journalist anywhere near it.

We don't write the headlines: Well-resourced publications have sub-editors and production staff who specialise in headlines. So when you commission us for a blog entry or article, it may well not have a headline on it - we will have anticipated this being written by someone on site. It's no problem if this isn't the case, but if we've asked 'do you have production taken care of' and you answer with a 'yes', we will get a little fractious when you ask why there is no standfirst and no headline in the copy. (standfirst: the longer bit that goes under a headline but is before the actual article starts).

We do this for a living: So we have bills to pay, so we really, really don't welcome people who think we can write something for thirty quid per 1000 words because we should be learning about this stuff anyway as part of our general research. If you want a professional job done, you need to pay a professional rate.

No you can't see copy before it's published: I still get asked that. Quite honestly the editor is the person commissioning me, he or she is my client and that's who gets first look at the copy. Why would you want to see copy before it's edited anyway? You don't have approval rights, but even if you did, if it's going to be cut about and rephrased in some cases by the subs, what relevance does the first draft have..?

> **"Don't ask a journalist to work for nothing. We have bills to pay and if we're freelance we have to sell, not give our time."**

Don't put up with this: when journalists are inconsiderate to PR people

I'm a journalist and as such I deal often with the public relations community. Contrary to popular bar-room tales, most of them are pretty good at what they do. It annoys me when I see it going wrong needlessly. Other people have written about incompetent PR people before and will no doubt do it again, but there are bad mistakes on our side too. Here are some of the chief offenders:

Assuming the PR industry exists only for us. I've actually seen journalists online complaining that PRs don't appreciate that their job is there for our convenience. Certainly a good PR will treat us as if we are the client, but we're not. They're not accountable to us, they have a separate employer, separate manager and separate objective. It's as if they were a business in their own right.

Assuming the PR people should know us individually. This will happen when there's a good working relationship of course, but it's not essential. After 20-odd years working as an IT journalist I still get asked who I am and who I work for. There are two very good reasons for this. First, several of the professional PR people who talk to me now were quite literally in nappies when I started in 1989. Why should they know me? Second, the fact that I may have written regularly for the FT in 2002 is of course deeply thrilling to me but many people who were still at school at the time see no reason to give a damn. Objectively neither do I. What I do now is going to be of much more interest. But a number of seasoned hacks are known to snap at anyone who dares ask.

Assuming journalists are independent and therefore 'purer' than PR people. I actually heard this from someone in PR once and he used the exact phrase – what I do, he said, was 'pure'. I explained to him that I wouldn't be writing about uninterruptable power supplies or mobile phone chargers unless someone was paying me, so although my 'slant' was on behalf of the reader rather than a particular client, my interest was still paid for and therefore commercial. I'm puzzled when fellow journalists get precious about this.

Review equipment should be kept whenever possible. When I was a young journalist there were a couple of wags in the office who'd always try to wangle a laptop (when they were expensive) and equally there were PR people who'd urge their clients not to ask for equipment back. There is no justification for this. OK, look, when I'm writing for my men's lifestyle blog at LifeOver35.co.uk and someone sends me a bottle of aftershave to sample, I can see it's a lot of fuss to get an incomplete bottle of niff back which they couldn't send out again anyway. But mostly, when someone sends you something to review, it's not your property. Capiche? (Of course a freebie is nice occasionally and I have been known to accept them - I just don't think it should be taken as a right).

It is acceptable to be rude to PR people. I come across this a lot. I'm aware of one occasion on which a journalist doing some media training actually reduced a PR person to tears and told her she was in the wrong job. Look, the fact that you're a rude sod who can't be bothered to treat someone with basic politeness tends to suggest you can't cope with the pressure of your job - therefore logically you're in the wrong position, not the PR person on the other end of the phone. I find "Thanks, but this one's not for me" terminates a call as efficiently as "No (SLAMS PHONE DOWN)" without intimidating anyone.

That said, if everyone else could carry on being a slob it would help me no end - I'll just continue to take all of the corporate assignments and media training that happen when you treat people reasonably.

The dreaded follow-up call

So I'm sitting down literally minding my own business (I write for a living and am working on a deadline so definitely minding it) and the phone goes. It's a PR executive.

The call goes:

He: Hello, I'm calling to follow up a press release I sent this morning about (NAMES CLIENT) and (NAMES SERVICE). I wondered whether you had any plans to feature it or whether you needed any more information.

Me: (LOOKING AT 60 EMAILS I'VE HAD TODAY) Actually, no.

He: (TOTALLY THROWN) I'm sorry...sorry, could you repeat that?

Me: No, no plans at all.

He: Oh. Er...well, if you do need anything...?

The thing is, that call was always going to go nowhere for a number of reasons Most of these have to do with the nature of the dreaded followup call.

Add value

Let's get two things straight. First, journalists are genuinely busy. The reason I get about 60 emails per day is that I am freelance; were I on the staff of one of the Nationals instead it would be hundreds. So putting in a 'Did you get the press release' call on the same day really, really isn't clever. In recent weeks I've even had people phone within two minutes of sending the release - so the response, reasonably enough, is that I haven't yet read it. The second thing is that we're miserable, self-important curmudgeons. Oh come on, we earn a living by getting our name in print, you think deep down we're modest people? So the chance to terminate a call by demonstrating we're too busy to talk is often too good to resist. Don't make it easy for us!

Here's a little secret. PR people can and do make effective followup calls no matter how much journalists say they hate them. However the content of that call is never "did you get the press release" or "did you want any information" - if we get that much unsolicited information each day of course we don't want any more.

Journalists sometimes wonder why PR people bother to make these calls. My guess as a journalist is that there are two reasons. One, they are very junior and their employers want to 'harden them off' by facing them with a load of hostile hacks. Two, they have a client standing over them demanding that the call goes in because the journalists haven't picked the release up yet. They are afraid they will lose the account and don't have the clout to stand up to the client and say 'we won't make this spurious call'.

To be more effective they actually need to look into the content of the call a bit more carefully. It's about adding value. There is really very little point in asking me whether I've received a release or whether I'm interested, if it hasn't already garnered a response. On the other hand, the call that goes "I sent this release yesterday: we now have a live customer you can talk to", or "I sent this release last week, we now have independent research from Forrester I can send over..."

See how that works? It is much, much more difficult for me to terminate that call as some sort of reflex - and if I had a call for every press release I received believe me I'd want to terminate them all as quickly as possible. If you're in PR and want to make that followup call, it's simple. Make sure you have something else to say. Add some value. I'll always try to be polite (something not true of all journalists) but if the call's going nowhere I'll shut it down pretty quickly.

> **"Before picking up the phone or telling your PR person to do so, make sure you have something more to say than 'did you get my release?"**

Know your journalist

OK, the year has got off to a good start with a morning's media training. It was a company I'd trained before, nice people, I liked it. Then I got back to the office and found the public relations missive from hell.

I do appreciate that people have to make a living and a few pages ago I highlighted practices from journalists which are unhelpful in the extreme. But it would help if PR people played the game too.

So I get this email. 'Dear Guy', it starts, denoting some sort of personalisation. 'I wondered whether you would be writing about (SUBJECT DELETED TO PROTECT THE GUILTY).'

No, as it happens I'm not.

'If so, you might want some comment from my client.'

Actually, no.

This is then followed by four paragraphs of comment on a subject on which I have no interest, about which I am not writing and even if I were, I would be highly unlikely to use the same overlong quotes that everyone else has presumably already received.

I honestly can't imagine what the desired result of that note was. If any PR people are reading and get traction from that sort of approach please do let me know, I don't mind being proven wrong.

But rather than scatter some unusable quotes to everyone, why not just phone five or six of us and ask whether we're working on anything in this subject area? You might at least get a decent conversation out of it, and once you've found out exactly what we're looking for you might even find you can help.

No, you can't see what I write before I publish

One of the longest-standing misunderstandings between journalists and our subjects is copy approval - people who want to see what we're writing before it gets published. Ninety-nine times out of a hundred or more frequently, the answer is a polite 'no'.

Sometimes people get quite uppity about this. One woman once told me she had entered the interview on the understanding that she would see the copy. I had to point out - again, politely - that an 'understanding' was something that exists between both parties, and needed to be established before an interview takes place.

There are a number of reasons we don't allow copy approval. Here are some that spring immediately to mind:

Ethics 1: equal terms. Very simply, if everyone doesn't get copy approval then nobody should. That's only fair. In terms of professional ethics, too, we're employed by editors and publishing houses. We are accountable to them, not someone else, and they will come down on us like the proverbial ton of whatsits if we show our copy to other people before they see it.

Ethics 2: Freedom of the press. Yes it can sound a bit pretentious. But this is a free country and we are allowed to say what we want. We'd better be accurate and to be able to substantiate whatever we say, but if I put in an accurate quote obtained honestly and you feel it's not in your interests, or if I put in a comment of which you don't approve but which is an honest opinion, that's perfectly permissable. Of course I should give you the right of reply but you may not censor it unless it's actually defamatory.

Practicalities 1: time. There is never enough time to get an interviewee to check through copy and adjust it to what they wish they'd said instead (which, incidentally, is not a reflection of what actually happened during the interview and therefore doesn't do the job as commissioned). I was once sent to the Abbey Road recording studios by the Radio Times to do an interview about a radio play being recorded there; I was specifically instructed not to talk to one actor in particular who would insist on copy approval. I interviewed Sir Derek Jacobi instead - ironically the younger actor would have benefited from the publicity much more (I was of course thrilled to interview Jacobi in the building in which the Beatles recorded Sergeant Pepper).

Practicalities 2: subbing. Sub-editors cut and expand for length. They rewrite for house style and sometimes for sense. Most are brilliant at this, although I've seen one or two exceptions. In other words the version you see, even if I do send you my draft, is not the version that will appear in print. So why bother looking at it?

Basic politeness. Some people just want to check articles for accuracy. What they don't realise is that this is pretty damned insulting - I've been in this job since 1989: of course I make mistakes, everybody's human, but someone who wants to see a draft of what I write before the editor is basically saying "I don't trust you to do your job". The fact that on the odd occasion an editor is daft enough to agree copy approval the draft comes back full of corporate guff and no longer to the correct length, having been introduced to a whole bunch of capitalisations and other elements not in house style (so the subs will remove it), barely seems to occur to anyone.

Journalists may allow you to check your own quotes. If it's a technically or legally complex issue they may even welcome written rather than spoken comment, or might run something past you to make sure it's actually accurate. Asking for copy approval on a whole article, however, is an open invitation to us to go and speak to someone else instead.

Now, did you really want to hand your opportunity to get coverage to the competition?

Media training and journalist ethics

A while ago I was asked to quote from media training - and also asked to confirm when I'd be writing about the client afterwards. I explained that I wouldn't. If the client was paying me directly I couldn't possibly pass myself off as someone with no vested interests so would not consider writing about them for several months. The PR person commissioning me dropped the session like a hot brick. He would only hire a media trainer, he said, if it would lead to direct coverage of his client. This was him doing his job, he said, and he was surprised I didn't understand.

Well, ten years in the media training business (first client Microsoft 2002) tells me he had some fundamental misunderstandings but here are two to kick off.

* First, a journalist can't possibly claim to be unbiased when talking about a company that is paying him or her. Therefore we have to keep a professional distance if we've done media training, commercial work like copywriting or speaking for someone - there is just no way we can sustain independence if we're accepting money directly. And our independence is all we have to sell.

* Second, from the PR's point of view, let's assume you get a journalist who'll bend that particular guideline and write about your client anyway. So they've done the training, they've negotiated a slot in a magazine, they've interviewed the client and written the piece. How on earth do you know whether the training has worked if you're paying the journalist direct anyway?

A wise journalist will keep his or her media training activities very separate indeed from the writing. To do otherwise may involve deceiving the editor and the readers about the nature of your relationship with the companies about whom you're writing. Your own self-respect should preclude that, and if it doesn't then the inevitable career damage that happens when it comes out is likely to be beyond repair.

So no, if you want me to media train your client I'm not going to promise to write about them in the papers immediately afterwards. But if the training's any good I shouldn't have to.

> **"Don't ask us to media train you then write about you – it's a clear conflict of interests."**

Professional Communicators and their communications

One of the irritations I get in my job as a freelance journalist, and something I try to address whilst media training, is when professional communicators don't understand the words they use. This, then, is the first in an occasional series on people who've approached me with the wrong thing. Yesterday I was approached with an "exclusive". Maybe you can guess the rest.

This has happened to me twice before. Yesterday and on the previous occasion the set-up was identical. PR exec got in touch and said there was a press day and offered me a slot for an exclusive interview.

OK, consider the word 'exclusive'. This can of course have different connotations. At an event it might mean everyone is wearing a tie. It may mean it's in a very posh hotel. To a journalist, however, it means one thing: nobody else has the story or interview. And if there's a press day, on which the executives or other interviewees are talking to a load of people, it's anything but exclusive.

On the first occasion I called the PR person and asked about this; she said any questions I asked would be exclusive to me (great piece of thinking on her feet but I think she knew this was baloney). Yesterday I emailed the guy and asked what was exclusive about this if loads of people were invited; he hasn't replied.

Total non-exclusive

The first time this happened to me was even sillier. In 1989 I was starting as a journalist and had interested my employer, Dennis Publishing, in putting out a 'poster magazine' of the new Indiana Jones film, *Indiana Jones and the Last Crusade*. I would write the text. This came out and I worked from printed materials.

The PR person had said, however, that she would try to get me some phone time for exclusive interviews with the stars, Harrison Ford and Sean Connery.

There is simply no way Ford, Connery or the studio system could ever have agreed to exclusivity, particularly for a small-circulation poster magazine as I was suggesting. It's actually a ridiculous suggestion. But that was the phrase she used.

It's really simple. An exclusive is a story, or at least an interview, that isn't available elsewhere. It gives a journalist or a publication a competitive edge because the rest haven't got it. If you can't offer one, nobody's going to be offended - just don't tell us something's exclusive when it's actually going everywhere. If I repeat the offer back to an editor and interviews appear elsewhere then I look a fool; if you use the word without knowing what it means and you're in PR, you look as if you don't know your job.

When PR people get it right

A few pages ago I highlighted some relatively poor practice from a public relations executive; now it's the turn of the good guys. It's so easy to carp when something is wrong, but here are some examples from my experience in which the PR industry and its members has got it spectacularly right.

RTFP (Read The Friendly Paper): Always try to have an idea of what you're pitching to. Numerous journalists including me have found themselves bemused when someone suggests an idea for a non-existent section of a newspaper or magazine. One colleague actually had a call from a PR person who'd biked something to a magazine which itself had closed three months previously, and the sender was most put out.

On the other hand I've had people pitching to, say, Unified Communications Insight, saying 'I see you run a case study every other week' - which tells me they've noted not only the content but the frequency. Human nature says that if they've done that much work I'll be inclined to be helpful.

Have an outcome in mind: I once had a complaint from an interviewee that after a reasonably positive piece I'd written, no new customers arrived. I was writing for the trade press at the time and the fact was that no end user/consumer types would actually have been reading. The PR and marketing people hadn't thought as far as 'what happens after we've got this coverage?' - had they done so, the chances are they would have targeted another paper in the first place.

A better example happened when a colleague asked me to speak at a trade show on his company's stand. The price for his offering was tiny and I asked how he made the expense stack up against the income; he told me his objective was to get the name out there so that's how he'd measure the results. He therefore had a good outcome because - wait for it - he'd set an achievable objective first.

Listen to the journalist: I accept the PR industry doesn't work for us and that a Guy-shaped story may not always be in their interests. But let me give you two examples. I once had a pitch from someone about a relatively new service their client was offering. I was writing something for the Guardian at the time and thought it might fit quite well; I said, what this needs is a customer to comment. The PR person said OK, fair enough, and did nothing more - in other words he wasn't prepared to go and ask whether there was a customer available, so he forfeited the Guardian coverage.

Persuade spokespeople to be available: One reason I've never wanted to go into PR is that executives in that industry must be so dependent on clients. And some of those clients assume that a PR person will simply produce favourable copy, they think they've delegated that activity, and this is wrong. The client needs to listen and to be available; when I'm calling people and leaving messages for a call back to get some comment, I'm likely to remember the ones who call back and in future not bother with the ones that don't. This means impressing the importance of calling back on your client, which isn't universally easy, but the PR people who manage it and become trusted advisors are habitually better than those that don't.

Understand how journalists work: People who call with an unexciting news story five minutes before the front page goes away are never going to get a result. People who take the time to ask whether there's a less bad time to call, when we put the inside news pages away so they can time their 'softer' news when we're in a receptive mood, will do better. People who complain about a headline (I've certainly had that) won't be as popular as people who understand journalists rarely if ever write headlines. It's a simple matter of finding out the working patterns of the people into whose magazines and websites you want to get your clients actually operate. Likewise if you don't own a trade magazine it's no use phoning the editor and telling him you're not happy with your story not appearing, or telling her you'd like a good story on the front page, maybe not the lead but don't put it somewhere rubbishy like page 4...no, seriously, I've seen this happen. We also have professional proofreaders so if you see any spelling errors in this blook they are not my fault.

That said, watch your phrasing. In my very early days as a freelancer I called a (female) monthly magazine editor I knew a bit, and knowing she'd have frantic press days I thought it best to find out whether I was phoning at a bad time. So I heard myself asking "Hi, I'm not sure whether this is a good time to call, where are you in your monthly cycle?"

Luckily she had a sense of humour!

Handle tricky questioning

Press interviews can be tricky and people often feel pressured into giving an answer for everything. They look at this famous clip of Jeremy Paxman interviewing Michael Howard – give it a quick YouTube search, Paxman asks the same question 17 times - and they worry it's going to happen to them:

In fact Michael Howard was a publicly-elected MP and Secretary of State; very few people are accountable to the public in this way. Many businesspeople will be unable to answer questions and they should give their reasons when declining them. Here are some examples:

You don't know the answer: I was once covering the launch of a mobile phone, one of the first to sync with Microsoft Outlook. I asked the CEO of the company when it would work with Microsoft Entourage, the Apple Mac equivalent, and he said this would be in "January". The following day I had a call from the PR company who organised the launch, sounding very sheepish; there was no plan at all for the phone to work with the Mac. He'd flustered, thought he ought to say something and - crucially - made something up. 'That will be coming in January,' he said, which was actually utter drivel. There were no plans at all for it to work with the Mac (which would have been more difficult at the time than it is now). Luckily the PR people got to me before anything appeared in public or it could have been quite damaging. "I will have to check", "Can I get someone to get back to you on that", all of these responses are fine.

It's not your department: So you're in tech support and I ask you whether your sales department is performing well. You give me an honest answer that says 'mostly but we have a few people coasting'. I'll leave you to guess how pleased your sales director is about that when it appears in print. Likewise if I ask about any cutbacks of which you're unaware, figures you're not sure you can publish. You speak about your area of the business or the business in general if you've agreed internally that you can do so.

You haven't been briefed: The classic example is when a journalist says something like "I hear you're about to make 50% of your sales department redundant" and you answer "No, only 25% are going" - and we have a confirmed story stating you're losing a quarter of your sales department, which you didn't want to tell us about. Clearly an accurate story is better than an inaccurate one but ideally, if you haven't been briefed to talk about something, "I'm not the right person to talk to about that, let me get our PR people to sort this out for you" is a good response. Make sure they do, make sure the facts aren't hidden, make sure anyone who's losing their job hears it from you rather than us. Note how the management of HMV survived mostly unscathed when they had to shut a lot of shops down – they were completely up front about what's going on and ensured communications were good, with well-briefed people handling inquiries.

It's confidential: Sometimes we'll ask for figures or customer names you can't disclose. If you can't help, say so. You don't work for us so it doesn't matter how much we want a confidential fact - we'll find it frustrating but ultimately that's our look-out.

You don't want to answer: This is of course trickier, you know the answer, there's no policy reason you shouldn't give it to us but you'd really rather be talking about something else. "No comment" always sounds defensive. There are strategies to get you out of trouble - one of which is to consider why a straight question is causing you such difficulty if the thing isn't confidential!

> **"If you don't know an answer, you can do a lot of damage by making something up."**

Avoid over-answering

Yesterday I had a public relations executive in touch, who'd heard I was writing in his client's area of expertise. He thought the client ought to be quoted and in fairness I thought he had a case. I asked whether we could get some quotes and he agreed immediately. I'd intended to suggest we should do a quick phone interview but was on a deadline so if he wanted to go and get something written that, I thought, would be acceptable.

If I'd had more time I would have insisted on a phone chat, in which I'd have been more in control and able to ask followup questions, clarifications and soforth. But for a few sentences 'written' would be OK.

He sent the comments through and hit the deadline, which was great. He actually sent through five paragraphs, which was great for me but an enormous disservice to the client, and it's worth sharing why.

Brevity keeps you in control

Think about it a second. I'm writing a newspaper or magazine article. When did you ever see an ordinary article (not an interview piece, which works differently) giving someone a quote five paragraphs long? Don't even bother checking - you haven't seen it, it's bad practice and makes for a difficult read, we don't cut and paste like that.

OK, so I'm a journalist, I can pick and choose and use the best quotes, the best sentences to serve my article and above all my impression of what my readers will need, right? Of course that's right. But if you're in PR, or are offering quotes to the press directly, you need to beware of that. It puts me in control, not you.

Suppose there's one key message, one massive point you wanted to get across. It's going to serve your share price, cement a partnership once it appears in print, whatever you want it to do (and you should be thinking in those terms, see the posting below on interviews needing an outcome for more on that).

And you've given me five paragraphs, in this case some 560 words (my editor is going to pay me for a total of 1000 and if I go too far over I don't work for her again). Clearly I'm going to exercise my right to choose which of those words I quote, which means you may not make an impact in the way you'd hoped. I might take a fancy to an anecdote you mentioned as an aside and use it as the most important part of my article. It will be accurate but it doesn't serve your marketing.

I might try to capture the flavour of the other stuff you've said but then you're down to my paraphrasing. I'll probably do a good job, based on 20+ years' experience, but if I'm condensing and replacing your words with mine there's room for misunderstandings and wrong emphases to creep in.

So whether you're being interviewed by phone, face to face or email, it's in your interests to deliver the answer you want me to quote, in as lively a fashion as you can, and then cut the waffle. If you or your client have only given me a few sentences they're likely to end up intact. It's a toughie sometimes, clients asked for quotes will go on at length for a while, but it won't serve them well. The professional, confident PR consultant will use the 'consultant' part of their job and steer the client towards brevity.

That said, the best over-answer I ever had was different. I opened with "Tell me about yourself and your company" – and he answered "Right, I think I know what you've heard!" and continued with a vehement denial that he'd been fired from his previous job or that there had been any bad blood between him and his previous boss.

Luckily that was in a media training exercise. If it had happened in a real interview I'd have been onto his previous boss very quickly indeed.

> **"Be brief with answers – the fewer words you give us, the more likely we are to use the ones you want us to."**

Don't give bad interviews

I've been a journalist now for 24 years full time and I've had some excellent answers to questions and also counter-questions from people who want to challenge me a little. That's something I relish.

I've also had a right bunch of charlies giving me some genuinely stupid answers. If you're a PR person, try to make sure your client avoids the following sorts of exchange - in all of these I'm GC, the interviewee is I:

5. The tactless

GC: So you make a good living out of selling these devices to corporate clients. What about smaller businesses?

I: What, the ones that buy how many...

GC: Say two or three units.

I: Bloody time wasters. Oh, were you writing this down?

4: The ignoramus:

I: *(A PR person who has phoned)* Hi, we're having a series of exclusive briefings for journalists -

GC: Hang on - how do you have a series of exclusive briefings?

I: It's exclusive in that only people who're there in person will get the interview, we won't be doing it by phone.

GC: So how many are invited to this exclusive?

I: About 17.

3. The megalomaniac:

GC: So, you're a small company -

I: I think you'll find we're classified as a medium sized business.

GC: How many people do you employ?

I: 20.

2. The megalomaniac (2, same company):

GC: So who do you target with your services?

I: Everybody. Everyone will need our service at some stage.

GC: Hang on, a company the size of Tesco doesn't market itself to everybody, and everybody needs food. Sainsbury's knows its own demographic from, say, Waitrose or Asda - so you can't -

I: No, you don't understand. We target everybody.

GC: How many people in your entire company?

I: 20.

GC: And you target...

I: Everybody.

GC: 60 million people in the UK?

I: Everybody.

1. The overconfident

GC: So, how do you attract customers?

I: We don't have to, people just call or email. They just arrive.

GC: That's unlikely...

I: No, really. People just turn up. We don't have to promote.

GC: OK, how many people are in your marketing department?

I: 15.

GC: Fire them, people are apparently just turning up...

Tell us what it's about

There's a company that's been sending me press releases for about two years now. It's usually about a new model of their product that's available for review. It will have a complicated serial number or something, and I will be told review units are available, please ask for further details.

You're wondering what they make. I have no idea. In two years of emails they have never bothered to say 'The XX/790 (a number I've made up, by the way, with apologies to anyone who makes a similarly-named product) is a phone/memory module/brand of whisky/shoe".

Of course I could Google, or I could email them back and ask. If I were all that concerned I'd have done both of those - but, call me juvenile if you like, I'm rather enjoying this. It's quite entertaining, guessing how long it'll be before they think of telling me what these wondrous widgets are. No kidding, it's been two years so far.

What needs to go into a press release

Seriously, there needs to be some basic content in a press release. Essentially it's who, what, why, when and where - as much of that as is relevant. Journalists get a lot of press releases and we're human, so get the basics into the first paragraph or some bullet points. We may not scroll past the preview pane in our mail program, we might not decide to click 'open' - so try to get as much info at a glance as you can.

There are some other points:

Large attachments, even in a broadband age, may not be welcome. And anyway, if we want a photo why not get us on the phone asking you for one? You're much better able to strike a rapport when we're talking to you rather than when we're reading a release.

Don't fret too much over the quotes in the press release - we're highly unlikely to use them. We know they've been worked, reworked and approved (and we know all of our competitors have the same quotes) - we'd rather talk to the client and get something conversational. A colleague was recently upset that her PR person had put all of her direct quotes into a press release rather than made them sound corporate and formal; the corporate/formal stuff, believe me, is not going to appear in our pages. (That said, when I made this point in a recent media training engagement the public relations executive confirmed that often the exact words are indeed used by the journalist – so make the quotes good and although I hate it when I see cut and paste quotes, it may well work).

Always put some sort of 'boilerplate' on the end- mine might say I'm an author, speaker and small-time stand-up comic; you or your client can eliminate any chance of people like me wondering what you actually do (see above) by having a standard sentence or two everyone uses, at the end of every press release, to confirm what it is you actually do.

> **"Don't assume we know your business. Explain everything in your press release."**

Being yourself

A media training candidate asked me this week whether he should tone his personality down for press interviews. He'd seen people laughing and joking around during trade shows and suddenly going all serious when talking to the press. Should he do that, he asked, or should he stay in 'friendly and approachable' mode?

My first instinct was that he should just be himself. Remembering which act you put on for the press and being consistent with an assumed character is likely to be disastrous, I reasoned. That said, there are exceptions; the sweary director who's going to make a bad impression no matter what he says unless he tones it down should certainly moderate his behaviour. But then we all change our vocabulary and attitude slightly depending on who we're talking to. If you phone me I will not speak to you as if I were addressing my child, and in turn I don't stand up in front of a clipboard and expect not to be interrupted for minutes at a stretch when I'm talking to my family - media training candidates I do just that. It's all about context.

There can be room for improvement, though.

The blank businessperson

A few years ago I was delivering leaflets to local businesses for my wife - she was laid up with flu, she worked at the time for the Council and they had to be delivered. I dropped one of them into a local shop - I won't say which one.

The owner was chatting away to a mate, happy as Larry. She realised who I was and she had a chat and a laugh - this woman, I thought, was engaging and would go places.

Then a customer walked in. He had a question.

It was fascinating in a 'what the hell just happened' sort of way. Her face fell into a deeply serious 'I'm only talking to you for the money' look. She mumbled her answer to him, she couldn't help, didn't have the stock, didn't suggest alternatives to what he wanted. No smile, just a factual 'I haven't got any of those, sorry' with no offer to help - and turned away to her chatting again immediately.

The shop is closed down now and of course she blamed the council for a lack of support. Engaging with everyone except her customer, though, was never going to make it work.

In the same way, if you formalise your approach to interviews too much, drain them of any trace of your personality and become the corporate droid, it's not going to work. By all means listen to the questions, answer honestly and completely within the boundaries of your job and try to bridge into other areas you need to promote, but keep some sort of energy going or the interview is dead.

Try not to be defensive

I've been listening to the Today programme on Radio 4 recently, as many journalists do. The questioning can be robust in the extreme but then they're often holding our elected representatives to account, so you can see why they'd do it. The responses vary from accurate and thorough to downright evasive. The worst, though, are the ones that fall into the 'defensive' category.

We can take it as read that the journalists are going to be downright bolshie and aggressive. It's what they do, and many - John Humphrys in particular but by no means alone - have been in their jobs for longer than their interviewees. They carry weight and they use it. But how clever does it sound when someone comes back with "Well, if you'd let me finish the answer" or "stop interrupting me..."

Would you do that in a conversation? OK, if you're a candidate on The Apprentice you probably would, but most of us are a little more polite. And there are a few easy verbal tricks to get you back to your original point:

"That's another important point I'll be pleased to address in a second. Just to finish the previous point, briefly..."

"I'll move on to that in a second but the listeners / readers / viewers should have the full answer to your previous question first"...

Then be brief and get to the new question as quickly as you can, unless you're trying not to answer it. Better yet, don't get into that sort of position in the first place: ask how long your slot is before the interview starts, and if you have only three minutes then understand every answer will have to be to the point. Ask for the first question before the interview starts so at least the first answer will be fluent to make a good initial impression.

Of course it's not the interviewer's job to make your life easier - but make sure the audience ends up thinking they're the aggressive one rather than you!

What to ask before an interview

So often I'm in media training sessions with internal or external PRs and a number of the usual tropes get trotted out (and there's nothing worse than a trotted trope). Ask who else is going to be in the article, they say. Get a list of all of the questions so you can be prepared, they demand. Find out when it's coming out, they finish.

In an ideal world, of course you would want to know all of these things. In fact I can tell you the answers: who else is going in - whoever I can get hold of, you may well be the first person to whom I've spoken. How do I know who else I'm going to come across or find? In terms of question lists, won't be reading from a script so I may not use the exact words but I'm happy enough to send a general brief. However, there is the frightening possibility you might say something more interesting than I was expecting and I'll pursue that instead. And in terms of when the piece is coming out, what, you think they tell the hacks?

Better questions

Those would be honest answers and I can't see how they're helpful. There are, however, a few scene-setters you can ask which will help you frame the interview in your mind:

How long do you need? You may not have set aside enough time for the interview. Asking in advance will help - and will also tell you if things are dragging on, giving you an excuse to reschedule (and do some more preparation) if things are getting difficult.

What is the scope of the readership? Ask this well in advance. I started in the trade press on MicroScope, a paper that went to the computer trade only. Well informed types were well aware we weren't interested in the bits and bytes but in the dealer margins and joint marketing budgets - our readers were commercial, not technical. Understand who you're talking to through the journalist and you should get a much better result.

What is the first question going to be? If you're going to be on TV or radio, no presenter should mind giving you their first question before you're in shot or on mic. The objective in asking this is to grab a few seconds to think before they ask it, so you're ready for at least one of the questions. That way at least the first thing the viewers or listeners hear from you won't be "Ummm..."

> **"Ask what the first question will be before the cameras roll"**

Always, always prepare

Some readers will be aware I've tried my hand at stand-up comedy from time to time. I mention this purely because someone asked me whether comics actually bother to prepare beforehand. The answer is: yes of course. You don't go into a full-fledged rant at a builder, which you revisit at the end to give it some structure, off the cuff. (The same bloke actually said to me that the thing about comedy was that if you had a certain Northern dialect you were funny and it just worked...you can imagine how useful I found that advice as a lifelong Londoner).

Interviews

Now, if people who want to have a laugh and are sympathetic to first and second time comedians expect their entertainers to be prepared, then interviewees for media interactions should be even more so. Except some of them aren't. I've media trained a few awkward people who genuinely believe they don't have to prepare for a media interview.

There's actually some substance to this. If I'm media training you, you're probably in a business (I don't specialise in celebrities or politicians), and you're the expert in your business, not the journalist. This being the case, it will feel as though there's no great need to do any research - as long as you've done a bit of brushing up on the figures why would you need to?

There are a couple of reasons. First, one of the big errors people make in media engagements is that they fail to speak consistently. I once attended the launch of a new watch, and the designer had moved manufacturing to Switzerland from the UK. I asked the sales director why they'd done this and he spoke about precision, he spoke about Swiss microengineering and how excited he was. I asked the MD, he shrugged and said 'because the customers want to spend an extra tenner on having a Swiss watch, the ones made in Hong Kong have passed the quality test too..."

This was a bit of a giggle of course, but if they'd compared notes beforehand they'd have agreed what the company line was. This was a harmless disagreement; others may be more substantial and play badly in the press.

Interviewees can also find they don't get any sales, mind share or whatever else they were hoping for from a particular engagement. What they don't always consider is that if they'd prepared in two stages they might have done better:

Stage one: Make sure the outlet you're going into has the right readers, viewers or listeners so that it can actually deliver - don't go into the consumer press expecting contracts worth millions, for example.

Stage two: Make a few notes and prepare some messages designed to deliver your desired outcome.

Then make sure you get those messages into your interview. Don't lie, don't ignore our questions, but it's a business conversation and any intelligent hack will expect you to be pushing your agenda a bit.

> **"Make sure each member of your company who is briefed to talk to the press sticks to the same story."**

Assess your objective

Only once you've got an objective/desired outcome and have assessed how realistic it is to achieve it from a particular outlet, you can start evaluating whether your press engagement is actually delivering.

Why do businesspeople do media interviews? To increase sales, to build profile and awareness, to generate buzz, some other reason?

I've seen it go wrong a number of times. Years ago - good grief, decades ago - when I was on the trade press, we'd always call someone for a "sanity check" quote for a news story. This would be an independent person, or a competitor, commenting on someone else's announcement, the classic

"Yes this will work because..." or "No, this was tried ten years ago and..." balancing comment.

Most people understood we were just after a contrasting view and decided whether or not they could help on those terms. I remember a few, though, who came out and said "I don't see how this is supposed to help my marketing", or "I don't see what commenting here gets my company, why are you calling me?"

Now, spelling your objections out this clearly to journalists isn't going to go down well. We don't work for you any more than you work for us, so we can at least respect that it's not our job to support your marketing function or get something specific for your company.

End game

Nevertheless, at least these guys were thinking about the likely outcome from their engagement with the press. So often people spend a lot of their time talking whenever we appear interested, getting quoted all over the place, but if their line managers asked them to justify the time in terms of business results they'd be hard pressed. It's very easy to be flattered by the attention and become known as a bit of a 'rentaquote' - journalists will love you but does it actually get your job done?

When you reach the position in which journalists are asking for some of your time, ask yourself (or a professional PR company) the following few questions before taking part:

- What is my desired outcome from taking part in this article?
- Is the readership, the viewer or listener profile, going to deliver this outcome?
- How much time can I spend on it and how can I be sure I get some messages that will deliver into it?
- How will I measure the success of this engagement?

Only then should you go ahead. Of course your objective may simply be to foster good relations with the press, and there's nothing wrong with that as long as you're aware that's all you're looking for. But next time, before you answer all of our questions slavishly, do ask yourself what you're doing with your time and why.

Never go off the record

When I started as a journalist in 1989 I was advised to try to get the "off the record" version of what was happening in a business. This seemed like a reasonable thing to do; I was inexperienced, looking for better and more exclusive stories than anyone else was getting and it was at least an honest request.

At this distance I'm not so sure and I don't go off the record any more. I always advise media training clients not to either. There are a number of reasons for this:

- You probably don't know the journalist in front of you very well. Why do you trust them to manage/remember what you wanted to see in print and not?
- Even if you do trust them, they're a journalist whose job is to report stuff. What is your objective in telling them something you don't want to see in print?
- Look at it from the journalist's point of view. Why do we want the pressure/hassle of remembering what you want

us to publish and what you don't - and given that we don't work for you, why are you expecting us to co-operate?

- Suppose you tell us something we think is so much in our readers' interests we break our word and tell everyone anyway - your only sanction is to say 'I wish I hadn't said that'. How is that going to serve your profile?

- Most importantly, what do you actually mean by 'off the record'? When I was new to journalism I spent a good couple of years quoting 'a source close to the company' when the marketing manager or someone didn't want to be attached to a particular comment by name. Hardly anyone ever complained, although I can see now I'd misunderstood 'off the record' completely - it means off the record, not unattributable.

But once again, why tell me something if you don't want it printed?

So here's the deal. If you're a work contact, if I'm contacting you as a journalist (my media training really is kept separate), then everything you say may be recorded, written down and generally used in articles. I will not, repeat not, do 'off the record'.

It sounds harsh and extreme at first - but see the way you always know where you stand with me after that?

"There is no such thing as 'off the record'."

The worst media training candidates

...are not the shy ones. People ask me whether it's difficult, bringing someone out of a metaphorical shell when they've pretty much pressed themselves into a corner and really, really don't want to be there or talk to the press. The answer is 'no'. That person has steeled himself or herself for the task, turned up in spite of any reluctance and above all understands he or she may not be a natural spokesperson. As long as a trainer is considerate these people can end up as a pleasure to coach.

No, the worst people to train are the ones that don't realise they have a problem. They are there, as one particularly poor-performing MD put it to me once, to support the others.

Here are some things I've seen in media training from candidates - try not to be one of them:

- The guy who assumed 'BlackBerrys off' didn't apply to him - nodding his agreement with 'mobile phones off' whilst checking his emails. Pretty please, try to be present in the room?

- The guy who spent the first 20 minutes of a session haranguing me about how trash the computer magazine on which I started out was. Believe me, if you do that you're wasting everyone else's time (and incidentally my time will cost you the same so you might as well make use of it).

- One MD who spent all of the practice interviews telling his colleagues how he'd sack them if they came out with the answers they'd just offered.

- The bloke who told me loads of stuff he shouldn't in an interview (more or less said 'don't buy any of my products until four months from now because there's a new version' when he had inventory to shift) and when his PR offered media training turned round and said 'Don't need it, I do amateur dramatics'. I'm still trying to work that one out.

- Not his fault, but there was a guy in France from a major blue-chip company who hadn't actually been tipped off that he was doing media training and treated the whole four hours as an interview about his encounters with the media, seeming quite affronted when I had a view or tried introducing any ideas or strategies. I still wonder whether the person commissioning the training had told him why I was there.

Actually the fact that I can remember five people over 11 years doing this tells you how well people generally respond. It's a great learning process for me, too; I almost always come out with some new insight into how people interact with the press and why, which keeps it fresh.

But if you're ever thinking of going for media training, please try not to be one of those five candidates. You might as well aim to get some value out of me!

The bridging technique

One thing a lot of people misunderstand about a press interview is that the journalist is not in sole charge of it – but they behave as if they are. So they fidget if you try to change the subject, they want you to address their questions and nothing else.

In no other business conversation would this be acceptable.

There are ways around moving the conversation on to your pet topic – or the subject you want to promote. The best of these is called 'bridging' and most of us do it in our daily lives. You can remember it by the initials A, B, C. It works like this:

Acknowledge

Bridge

Continue

So I ask you about something not in your comfort zone. Let's say: "I hear your margins are really tight and profits are therefore down by 50%."

You don't know whether I've heard any such thing. I could well have made it up. Or I have one of those journalistic sources, who may be a disgruntled employee, it may be an unscrupulous competitor or a supplier, or someone entirely different but you haven't been briefed about it.

So you acknowledge that I've spoken. You don't confirm anything but you Acknowledge the question. Something like:

"Profits vary all the time..."

"Profits are confidential but..."

Then use a Bridging phrase, like:

"What we're focused on is..."

"What really matters to our customers is..."

And then Continue with your content. So I might ask: What about profits dropping 50%? And your answer might be "Profits vary all the time, what we're really focused on is our new customer service initiative..." and soforth.

Nothing's fool proof and it won't work every time. But most of the time it's worth a try.

"Bridge into your comfort zone subject."

Journalists and the freebie culture

There was an excellent piece on the Press Gazette's site the other day, touching on something I mentioned in this blog a couple of entries ago. I was talking about relations with PR people and in the Press Gazette John Dale has been fulminating over journalists and their dependency on freebies. This bears some more discussion - and it's not as clear-cut as Dale would have you believe.

First let me state that I'm not in favour of the extremes of the culture he describes. Journalists insisting that they be taken out to a good restaurant or else they won't meet a PR client, journalists demanding free goods or travel, are bad things. I'm aware of an editor (this is a second-hand story) who regularly told her PA to get a copy of the latest box set she fancied sent over to her; the fact that the magazine didn't actually cover DVD reviews barely registered.

This is clearly wrong. However, there are areas in which some leeway helps make the system work. A few years ago I was writing a lot about gadgets - less so now as I found the rates didn't add up. Nonetheless, when you're writing about computer games, 3D TV and hand-held devices, the idea that you can only function if you buy your own upgraded TV set (four figures at the time), one of each sort of games console (Xbox, PS3, Wii and perhaps a gaming PC, another grand gone), one of each flavour of mobile phone...you can see that you'd have to earn a great deal in order for your business to be viable.

So I asked for loans of the right equipment and got them. I'm still grateful to the companies that furnished me with these long-term loans (as the euphemism has it - of course they could ask for them back anytime but I rather suspect they won't). They facilitated the work. Likewise, on the budgets available to the newspapers and magazines (blogs probably more so) high-end restaurant reviews and luxury hotel reviews simply won't happen without the companies donating suitable accommodation.

Independence

The trick is for the journalist or blogger not to bias their copy. That's the bit the public sees. The other trick is not to let the fact that people seem to be offering you freebies left, right and centre to go to your head. The sense of entitlement that creeps up on formerly idealistic young journalists when someone is putting luxury accommodation and catering in front of them on a regular basis is bound to turn a few heads.

The effects aren't just antisocial to those around them, who're annoyed by the "do you know who I am?" attitude mentioned in the Press Gazette piece, odious though this is. The recipients themselves start to feel as though eating out three times a week is normal, everyone has loads of nice holidays and a new watch (or whatever) twice a year. Someone once described journalists to me as having a middle class mentality, upper class aspirations and a working class income. So when the goodies stop there are some who find themselves trying to treat themselves to more of the latest iPad, Michelin starred restaurant and so on - on a credit card they will find very hard to pay off. They honestly end up with the impression that this is normal.

One underlying issue is that journalism as it stands is pretty underfunded. In other cultures the hacks insist on paying their way; you won't find many American journalists accepting flights or accommodation. In the UK, very few of us could get to events like the Consumer Electronics Show (CES) in Las Vegas in January unless someone else is subsidising us, and this includes staffers. This has been broken for some time and predates recessions; when I was on the trade press in the 1980s it was routine to expect someone else to pick up the tab for a trade show, and they did it. Let's not pretend that the PR industry hasn't been fairly complicit in this for as long as it's been happening.

And why shouldn't they be? If it gets their client the coverage they're paid to find, good luck to them. It's incumbent on journalists and bloggers, though, to make sure they accept only the essential freebies, without which they couldn't work. The fact that this should tell them they have a serious sustainability problem in their business is a longer term issue and a worrying one.

> **"Don't offer journalists bribes, only the lousy ones will accept them. Unless there's someone from Rolex reading."**

Section 2:

Social media and your profile

budgets
feel the
squeeze

SAVE

ely to pay

worth

plan

fits

$210m
$427m $439m $425m $453m
$578m

Rising de

home

Other people's playgrounds

Social image sharing site Instagram is going to start helping itself to people's rights to their pictures - this is alarming and we're all going to die, apparently. Or something. The papers this morning seem to have the tone rather than the substance of what's actually happening.

Essentially, as of 16 January, Instagram will be able to sell anything you've made public and not cut you in on a penny. This is in line with its now-parent company, Facebook. People are annoyed: today's Metro carries a quote from a user who's said this will be Instagram's death knell

Now, before we get too heated about this, let's bear one major, major factor in mind: we don't own Instagram. The company lets us in for nothing.

it's their network

This is a theme I've visited several times whilst presenting on social media. The new or not-so-new networks have effectively trained us to become dependent on stuff that isn't ours.

Say you need a place to work for a while and a friend who owns a business offers you a little rent-free desk space. You go and work there by all means, but you never question that their rules apply. And if their rules change you accept that. If your friend says there is now a need to get money from everyone who uses the service you might pay, you might withdraw, but you're unlikely to go screaming about how unjust it all is in public.

Facebook, Instagram, Twitter and the rest are similar in that you're working or playing in their space, but different in that offering this space is all they do. It's up to them to make this financially viable. So yes, they change their terms when the existing ones prove unprofitable.

And yet people assume that because these are 'social' companies, the user has the right to demand that changes don't happen and do the screaming-in-public thing. It is a fact that if you own a computer and have an Internet connection, thanks to Google, Spotify, LinkedIn and others you can have:

- An office suite through Google Docs
- Music in the background while you work from Spotify
- Photo storage and sharing through Flickr

- Business networking through LinkedIn
- Personal networking through Facebook

I could carry on, there's plenty more. None of this stuff will cost you at all. The problem is that giving it away for free is not sustainable for these companies. They clearly have to make money to pay for staff, premises etc. - the terms and conditions are in the most literal sense their business.

Sometimes they have to change them because the previous set didn't deliver the cash they were hoping. So we get LinkedIn deleting its "LinkedIn Events" app, to the consternation of many event organisers, because it didn't work for LinkedIn. We get Tungle deleting its shared calendaring because selling up to BlackBerry made more sense (I got caught with that one myself - you'll notice my e-media training service on my website has a video of me exhorting everyone to look at my Tungle diary to schedule phone appointments; Tungle withdrew the service within a fortnight of the recording), and yes, Instagram tightening up its terms and conditions.

They're allowed to. The networks are their property. If we don't like the terms we're under no obligation to use them. And if we want to complain when a service changes, is withdrawn or tries to monetise the content, we need to start thinking about paying for it rather than freeloading.

> **"If you're using someone else's network, they set the rules."**

Untrackable coverage

An odd question has just come up in an online forum. Someone is recruiting a journalist to write web pieces for them and they're asking how, since one of the candidates has been in print only, it is possible to find out how well-read their articles were, how long people spent looking at them and soforth. In other words the question is "how do I apply Google analytics when the words are on paper only?".

The answer, to me very clearly, is that you can't possibly. Before the Internet became pervasive - call it up to 2007 or thereabouts - I'd been writing for the Guardian and others for ten years or so. And yes, I very frequently suspected that most of the readers would disregard the supplement and skip to the TV, sports, politics or whatever other pages were on offer. That didn't affect my writing; I'd been commissioned to create something informative and engaging - and if it had my name on it, and was going into the National Press, it was going to be good.

The analytics the web can offer are unique to the electronic media. The sort of attitude they're starting to promote may become pervasive.

Is SEO helpful?

As I said above, I wrote assiduously for supplements - still do - in the full knowledge that only a subset of readers would even look at them. It's the job as far as I'm concerned.

But here we had someone who not only wanted to recruit based on the ability to attract clicks, but appeared baffled that it wasn't possible to do something similar on paper. It could well be that the culture is changing and the whole industry is going to go that way.

Let's accept that writing something nobody will read is a bit self-indulgent and a waste of time. I do wonder, though, whether stuffing a piece with keywords and structuring it for faceless search engines is actually any less so. You can end up with something very formulaic and quite dull - a mechanical ad-get piece which pays its way but inspires no thought or action on the part of the reader.

My own hope is that quality writing and a distinctive voice will have some way to go yet before SEO and "how many clicks?" takes over as the sole criteria for recruiting journalists. For an incoming generation, though, my view may start to look increasingly alien.

Mistakes people make on social media

OK, this social media thing's been going for long enough for people to have got the hang of it. But I still see people making the same old mistakes, so here's my take on them:

Self-promotion. I get it, I really do. I'm self-employed too and nobody else does my publicity, which is why you'll see me

Tweeting, Facebooking or Linked-In-ing about stuff I'm doing that I find interesting (and let's be honest, when I want to make people aware I'm involved in media training, broadcasting or whatever other sort of work I want more of). But on Facebook and LinkedIn discussion groups you need to go beyond that and really take part. People will remember what you said if you've replied interestingly to something much more than if you just announce your own seminar, workshop or whatever every time.

Irrelevance. An extreme example here would be yesterday when I joined a professional group on LinkedIn for a project on which I was working and found the first entry was about weight loss. OK, that's an extreme spammy example, but how many times have you seen a discussion thread hijacked so someone can get a point in about their business? This can annoy and is unproductive, but there's also a flipside:

Excessive moderation. If you're in charge of an online community of some sort you have to let it ebb and flow a bit. I've certainly seen interesting threads stopped because a heavy-handed moderator comes in and says "We weren't discussing how to negotiate a contract, we were discussing the grocer's apostrophe, so stop talking about this business stuff at once" - or words to that effect. Conversations do change and move about, in the flesh and online. Try to stop them and you risk looking like the five year old stamping his or her foot and shouting "You're not listening to MY bits!"

Constant pitching. Again, as a self-employed person I try to be vigilant about this one and probably fall foul of this more often than I'd I should when funds are low. But if someone on a group asks "do you know anyone who can help with X" you're actually much better off recommending someone other than yourself, improbable though it may sound. Everyone in that group is a potential lead or referrer for you if you make the right impression, and being generous with recommending others sends out some very positive signals indeed. I have a rule that on Fridays I actively look for leads for other people, and yes of course I'm hoping some of them will be able to reciprocate, but it's not obligatory. Play the long game and your online reputation will increase and so, I strongly suspect, will other people's inclination to recommend you in turn.

Dead-end and clunky Tweets, Facebook entries etc. Two things I try never to do on Twitter are lead people to dead ends or oversell my own stuff. An example of the first would be a writer I met once, liked, engaged with and followed on Twitter. I found that just about everything she said on that medium led to a blog entry or page on her site that said nothing more than "Book my course". There is nothing wrong with this as the end game but you have to add value first. Tweeting "Want more sales as a speaker?" is fine, but when I click through I need to find more than a statement that everyone is struggling so I need to book. A few bullet points, a couple of ideas I can use for nothing and I will be much more inclined to use your service - if I click through and find I learn nothing until I've paid you then sorry, I'm not going to go any further.

'Clunky' isn't as bad but it's annoying. A couple of writers I know and like are in the wince-making habit of highlighting often excellent blog entries they've written and saying "Worth re-reading" or "Interesting post" or something like that. Rule no. 1 of writing is that if you have to tell me your work is interesting, it probably isn't. If you've been telling people how interesting your stuff is and can track how many people come and read it, try spending a week just telling them the subject and see whether the numbers go up or down.

Are all your connections actual connections?

I've just re-connected with someone on LinkedIn. He's the guy who took the photo on the front page of my website, and very good I think it is too although it's going to need updating soon (on the minus side I'm greyer – on the plus side I'm about two stone lighter, and counting). Of course there was nothing on the 'how do you know this person' list that LinkedIn furnishes to specify that we hadn't actually met but he'd taken my picture; likewise when another colleague spoke at a conference and offered to connect with anyone who was in the audience, you can't actually select anything that specific in the list of reasons you're connecting with someone.

For people who aren't on LinkedIn, it works when you connect only with people you know and trust. So if you want to make contact, you find the person by searching then pick 'We worked at the same company', 'We've done business together' or whatever your connection actually is.

The catch-all, and the reason I was able to get in touch with my photographer and my conference speaker, is the category of 'we are friends'. This enables you to contact just about anyone. And it works, both people have responded positively although at least in the case of the photographer we've never actually met.

The problem with this approach is the amount of people I get (and it's the same for others) contacting me at random, putting 'friend' down to get round the system and generally pretending we know each other. In my first social media book I do invite people to get in touch so that's fair enough; on various LinkedIn groups, however, I'm starting to detect a certain resistance. Yesterday in a journalist group a member was complaining with some vehemence about this and I can understand why - he didn't know any of these 'friends' and the whole thing about LinkedIn is that it's supposed to be a trusted network, through which people introduce you to their connections, not a free-for-all.

I could see over time that LinkedIn will start to lose value if it doesn't do something to address this. What does everyone else think - has this 'six degrees of separation' ethos all but disappeared on LinkedIn, or was it an inappropriate idea in the first place?

Don't try to manipulate the blogger

As well as blogging here I run a small men's blog called "LiveOver35". That is, it's a small blog on men's lifestyle, not a blog for small men. Anyone who's met me will comment that even after losing a stone and a half over the last 12 months, I don't really qualify.

So I happily take receipt of samples, the latest being a shower gel/eau de toilette combo box set. I give it a decent write-up as it deserves one.

Then I get a note from the PR. It's lovely, they say. But could I add a sentence that says "[CLIENT] is a great place to buy Valentine's gifts at a fraction of the usual price" please.

Independence

Well, funnily enough, no I couldn't. I've had this before on the blog; people send in a note that says "this is great but you haven't put a picture of the product in" or something.

OK, so here are some blogging basics for the marketers:

- Bloggers, like journalists (and some like me are both), are independent. You might consider advertising, you might sponsor a post, in which case you get to put some corporate messages in, but aside from that this is our playground, not yours.
- We don't work for you. Of course if you get a good review you'll think it's a successful piece of marketing, and that's what it is. But you do not, repeat not, get to play with our phrasing - we may be accountable to a boss or ourselves (and of course the readers), but as long as we're accurate and non-libellous we're allowed fair comment.
- Even if we'll take guidance - maybe a bit of help with the description of a scent, for example - very few of us will accept straight marketing statements from you. Arguably it's our job to cut right through those and give the readers a straight opinion.

And the straight opinion was pretty positive in this case.

Of course the picture is distorted by a small minority of bloggers who themselves don't have a clue; when I started LifeOver35 I was struck by just how many men's lifestyle blogs simply cut and pasted press releases completely verbatim, which was and is ridiculous.

But please, if you're a PR person pushing a product or service either to bloggers or journalists, never lose sight of our independence. The bad impression you'll make is hard to undo later.

> **"Journalists and bloggers are allowed to use whatever phrasing they want as long as it's not libellous."**

When bad publicity becomes worse publicity

A few weeks ago I visited a cafe in our area. It was terrible; the 'hot' sandwiches took half an hour to arrive and were cold in the middle, we ordered two coffees and a single one turned up after 20 minutes, followed by the staff arguing about whether we'd ordered one or two. At 2pm they had run out of fruit juice for my daughter.

You can imagine I wasn't best pleased. And I always try to leave a few thoughts on where I've been on TripAdvisor - I've given some outlets a glowing review, really - so I did so. I didn't expect the owner to add me to his Christmas card list on the strength of it but it was an accurate reflection of what we found.

Thing is, the owner got in touch. And he didn't respond in public, just sent a sniping note by private message on TripAdvisor. First he criticised (rightly on reflection) my assumption that Cuban cuisine would be anything other than an offshoot of European - fair enough. He claimed the sandwiches were the same as you'd find in any other cafe (although he also insisted they were authentic Cuban so there's some inconsistency there); he told me I need to be concerned about the fact that he has only two grills and two members of staff on Saturdays (which is the customer's problem because...er...) and repeated in capital letters "WE ARE NOT A RESTAURANT".

If I'd been considering going back for a second try I'd have avoided it like anything after that. So, social media author hat on, what do you do about hostile reviews? In fact what have I done about them when they appear on Amazon about my previous books?

Dealing with hostility

My first book on social media has, at the time of writing, 54 reviews on Amazon, average four stars out of five. Clearly I'm happy with that. There are one or two one-star reviews. I deal with this in a number of ways.

First I ask who stuck my head over the parapet and allowed these people the right to comment. Once I accept that the answer is 'I did', I can't really complain when someone a) gives an honest account of what they think and b) happens to hate my writing style. It's allowed. On that basis you have to go into any engagement first respecting the other person's right to express a view, and second determined that you're going to exit from this looking professional.

So, ranting, capital letters, loads of excuses and expecting that people should take your circumstances into account are big no-nos. A week ago I did a five minute stand-up spot that went OK but not brilliantly. I didn't stand in front of the audience saying 'Come on, it's only my fifth gig'; I took it on the chin, took the applause on offer and thanked the organisers for the opportunity.

Likewise I've never responded defensively to criticism of my books. If someone posts a five star review and puts their real name up I try to find them on social media and drop a note of thanks; if someone puts a one-star review up then I read it carefully to see whether there's anything I can learn. One person gave me three stars and pointed to one area that needed improvement (I'd been glib about working with overzealous web designers who'd put their wishes above the client's needs) - on balance I thought he was right, so I left a note on Amazon thanking him and saying I'd deal with this in any future editions. Everyone can see this. Another person criticised the edition that came out in early 2011 (so, researched and updated in 2010) for overlooking certain elements of social media. In fact these were developments since 2011 so I commented and said so – but confirmed that people should indeed bear in mind that this was a 2010 update of a fast-moving industry.

If you're really stung by criticism on a social media site then here are a few suggestions which may help:

- Keep any commentary in the public domain - if the review is factually unfair in some way you want everyone to see it. And if you wouldn't put a comment in public, why would you do it in private?

- Don't rant. Politeness is everything - your underlying objective may be to undermine the credibility of your critic; you won't manage this if you're the shouty one.

- Less is more: if my correspondent had wanted to deflate me very simply he could have said "Sorry to hear the food wasn't to your taste; I'm from Cuba and can assure you of its authenticity". And wham - I'd have been dead in the water. Instead a private message accuses me of not caring about the community, not supporting local business, which are easy charges to dismiss.

- It's probably best not to comment at all unless there's a factual inaccuracy. I've certainly left most of the one-star reviews alone on Amazon; the writers are fully entitled to their view, I'm not going to change their mind and I know I'll look an idiot if I start engaging in that way.

- Try to find out a little about the person leaving the comments. If it's on Amazon or TripAdvisor you can click their name and see whether they make snidey comments about everyone - or whether they're usually pleasant. My correspondent could have found a review of another cafe in the area which would have told him I'm generally quite positive with my comments. The cue then is to consider the new hostile review as a learning experience. Then work damned hard to ensure the positive reviews outweigh the negatives - the thing about social media is that people will listen to the larger numbers.

And don't whatever you do take a piece of criticism of a business personally - it's not about you, it's about a customer's reaction to your goods or services. And even if you take it personally, don't let it show in your reaction!

"Snapping in public at bad reviews never, ever looks good."

Section 3:

Your audience – speaking in public

attracts

attractive

sales

pay best

worth

banking on

find savings

Gold price

five-year

When hardly anyone turns up

Day one of the Business Startups Show 2012 in London, hour one indeed, and there is a trickle of people coming in. The queues are building up outside and I'm due to start speaking on one of the stands which has a small theatre, and I'm on at 10.30 (doors opened slightly late, just after 10).

Inevitably people are finding their bearings. Nobody, repeat nobody, is in the audience yet. So we postpone a little and by 10.45 we have one person. Inevitably you have to ask: is it worth speaking to an audience with a prepared presentation if you find you can address the audience by her first name?

The answer, we decided pretty quickly, was "yes" and we were proven right. Passing audiences who don't know they're audiences will stop and consider what's going on; we grew to 8 people seated and another 10 or so standing on the sidelines fairly quickly. It's still not a massive number but we only had seating for about 30 - my client, Telnames, was being very realistic about their prospects of attracting big numbers at a busy show with so many distractions.

Inevitably it was less about the numbers than about who was actually there. By the end of the presentation I'd made contact with one audience member from Sri Lanka who'd read my books and wanted to meet me - it's always brilliant when something like that happens. I also had another audience member coming to ask whether I would be interested in speaking for her organisation (and later did so, earning a small fee). This is my idea of half an hour very well spent indeed.

None of which would have happened if we'd abandoned ship because of poor early signs. So if anyone's ever thinking of scrapping something because not enough people have turned up, remember:

1. If you have a contract and are being paid for your time, you deliver the presentation for which you've been commissioned, regardless;

2. If there is significant 'passing trade' you may well pick up an audience as you go. In fact, if you're any good then you ought to find people willing to listen.

3. Even if only two people turn up, they might be the right two people.

None of this stuff will work if you scrap your presentation - so whatever you do, keep going!

"An audience of one person can work if they're the right one!"

What happens at a media training session?

I've been out today - media training for computer security company Trend Micro. I don't disclose my clients without permission - they may want to keep an external trainer's involvement confidential - but within hours they'd put this on Twitter:

@guyclapperton Thanks from everyone here at Trend for a great media training session today! ^FC

— Trend Micro UK (@TrendMicroUK) December 3, 2012

So that's fine. People do occasionally ask me what you get when you hire me as a media trainer for half a day. Ideally you get more confident in front of the press as your desired output and make any interviews more productive for both sides. A few strategies to get yourself out of trouble and to introduce your topics unobtrusively if the journalist isn't asking the questions you'd hoped for, and above all you get interview practice.

Today's session took three and a half hours on the client's premises. Most of the candidates had little or no experience of press interviews but by the end of it they were batting questions they couldn't answer out of the way and turning queries around to subjects they could speak about comfortably. Here are a few general hints:

- If you don't know the answer to a question from a journalist, you're allowed to say so. What do you think's going to happen? It's not as if you work for us.

- You're fully entitled to prepare for interviews - even if that means telling us you're about to nip to a meeting or the loo when we call unexpectedly, to give yourself five minutes to make a few notes on what you need to say.

- If something isn't in your area - maybe you're in sales and we're asking about financials - say so. Refer us back to your PR people or to the right person by all means - but don't let us pressurise you into commenting out of turn.

Losing marks for hesitation

Probably the weirdest thing I've ever been asked by anyone who's thinking of speaking in public or being interviewed is "how do I eliminate the errs and umms". This tells me a number of things. First, they have never seen me speak. I'm full of those things, all the time – I do it on radio, I do it on TV and I do it on stage in person. My media training sessions, which typically last four hours, would be stilted and artificial if I worried about those trimmings too much.

People are intelligent and filter out a load of stuff. You'll be amazed at what they don't hear – in every day conversation we hesitate, we repeat, we umm and err a whole lot and people don't register it. Getting hung up on that will add to, rather than subtract from, your nerves. Anyone in any doubt should just look at how 2012 was for Boris Johnson, Mayor of London; he makes a virtue of being slightly shambolic, appears unable to get a full sentence out but we all know what he stands for, whether we agree with him or not, and his personal popularity is through the roof.

To my mind people are better concentrating on the content – what they're actually going to say, and never mind how they're going to say it. Key to this is preparation. Have a note of a few points you want to make, and always, always start with the audience as your focal point rather than what you might want to offer them.

This can't be overstressed. The audience comes first. For example, yes of course I want people to read this and book me as a speaker or speaking coach; however, if I'd said that in my first sentence very few people would be reading by this fourth paragraph. I have to give you something of value. Concentrate on the people to whom you're talking and what you need them to take away before anything else and you're likely to have a successful event on your hands.

It happened to me a couple of weeks ago. I'd pitched the idea of a training/mentoring session for public relations executives and contract publishers on how journalists like me can misunderstand corporate assignments – our interpretation when they ask for 'independent' writing, for example, why we won't write headlines unless prompted (not usually part of the journalist's job), and soforth.

I thought this would be useful for people in PR and contract publishing. Before the event, though, I dropped a quick email to the participants and asked whether there were any specifics they wanted covered. Four of them wrote back and asked about how to make press releases stand out, whether journalists used social media – in other words, nothing to do with the course as pitched. So I prepared around what they'd asked for rather than what I'd intended, and within an hour of finishing one of them had put a note on Twitter about how much they'd enjoyed it. It wasn't the session I'd planned to put together (it was a load easier for me, as it happens) but it turned into a better one with happier attendees.

So, prepare, find out about your audience, talk to them in advance if you can. Then accept that they're as keen to have a good presentation as you are – they're really not the enemy – and the basis for a lot of your nerves will go away.

P. S. The other thing to bear in mind is that the opposite to 'nerves' is 'overconfidence' – anyone who arrives at a venue without any trace of doubt that they'll deliver something of value and precisely what the client wants is probably suffering more than a little arrogance. Let those remaining nerves spur you on to do better rather than hold you back and you should be fine.

> **"Listen to your audience and deliver what they want/need, not what you happen to want to offer"**

Booking a speaker and why I won't be pencilled in

I fell out with a client a couple of years back. It started badly; he called and asked whether I'd speak on my then new book, "This Is Social Media", to his clients. I quoted a fee, he explained that his was a small business so he wouldn't be paying that (lesson one: walk away at this point) but since I didn't have anything to do on the evening he mentioned six months ahead, we agreed I'd 'pencil this in'.

The rest of this story, if you haven't got much time and want to get to the point, is about why I will never 'pencil anyone in' again.

Months went past and I heard nothing. No confirmation, no contract, and if I'm honest it slipped my mind completely. I get a lot of 'could you do such and such a date if the opportunity was right' questions and many of them just go away because the executive in charge hasn't been able to get the budget, they haven't been able to sell enough places so cancelled the event, or whichever variation of those factors militates against going ahead.

So I had another offer from someone wanting me to speak in five European countries, at a much more sensible rate of pay, including the date about which I'd heard nothing for four months. OK, I said, I'd be delighted and indeed this turned out to be one of the happiest professional engagements I'd ever had.

A week before the 'pencilled in' date, however, my name came up in a Tweet from the earlier client. Looking forward to hearing @guyclapperton at my event, was the substance. 'You all set?' it asked. I had to break it to him that in the absence of any word I'd assumed the thing wasn't going ahead and had other arrangements.

The email I had within ten minutes was plain abusive. He was clearly furious; he'd spent his own money publicising the event and didn't realise I'd need my hand held like a baby. You get the idea. I responded calmly, pointing out that he hadn't booked me firmly, there had been a very loose agreement, neither confirmation nor contract, and I'd assumed he'd be in touch. He didn't reply.

Phrasing

The lesson I've taken away from this is never to allow ambiguity into a negotiation. To me, 'pencil in' means 'be aware something may happen on this date and you'll probably have confirmation soon'. To the client - or perhaps I should say non-client as I didn't work for him in the end - it clearly meant 'booked'. It's actually a useless phrase and I won't 'pencil in' anyone any more. I'm either booked or not. I also have an agent who's good at negotiating contracts and getting proper commitment from both sides - this won't be happening again. Letting ambiguity into the arrangement was at least 50% my responsibility.

The client could also have learned something I hope. First, use meaningful terms in negotiations. 'Pencil in' really doesn't mean anything until you've confirmed it so don't use it. Second, send a contract or emailed confirmation.

Third, if things go wrong by all means write an angry and abusive email. Then delete it and write something more constructive instead. Ask where things have gone wrong even if you're convinced you're in the right; communications exist between two parties and you can probably improve your processes when an arrangement falls apart.

Meanwhile anyone wanting me to pencil something in, sorry. I welcome bookings for speaking on media matters, social media and after dinner speaking and will commit wholeheartedly as long as the client does, too; agreeing to maybe doing something probably in a few months' time and hoping you'll remember to confirm except you're expecting me to do the chasing is not an arrangement into which I can enter.

> **"Be precise about what you mean when booking someone – don't use vague phrases that people can interpret in different ways."**

Adding stand-up to your armour

So I'm a serious business speaker. I am a Fellow of the Professional Speaking Association, I've had four figures for a presentation before now. And this evening I will be standing in the basement of a pub in London, unpaid, hoping that people will laugh at some material I've written. I wonder why myself, sometimes.

I do it for a number of reasons. First I really, really like the people. I fell in with the guy who masterminds these evenings, Tim Dingle (who wrote Harry Enfield's 'Tim Nice-but-Dim') at a Professional Speaking Association gathering on putting humour into your presentation. I've never had a problem doing this but wanted to keep it a bit more under control Anyway, there was an offer of a followup one-day workshop after which you'd get to do a five minute open spot at a comedy club.

I believe you should never get to 50 and regret not having tried something, so I signed up. The first course was great - loads of other PSA members there. I couldn't make the performance date so I did a second course - fewer PSA members but I'd got to know some other people and they're great. Loads of people there for different reasons; the guy who couldn't go on stage before he worked his way into a bit of stand-up, the bloke who has serious potential, Tim acting as a facilitator and ringmaster. On my first attempt in front of an audience I forgot my lines; the second was better, and tonight? Who knows.

My attempts at comedy have become a bit disengaged from my initial purpose if I'm honest. Sure, I pick up a few techniques and tips for dealing with an audience, and I get a bit of work because people know I do this - but it's long since become an end in itself. I love it, even if I'm only just beginning to find where my feet might be. It's brilliant, brilliant fun and occasionally when you get a laugh in the right place it's one of the best buzzes you'll ever find.

I'm utterly hooked and would recommend Tim's course and a bit of performing afterwards to anyone.

Learning from the greats: The Stranglers on business speaking

I went to a gig on Easter Sunday - I saw The Stranglers at Croydon's Fairfield Hall. They were pretty damned stunning and I thought, why not see what I can apply from them to my own presentations? (My colleague Alan Stevens wrote a piece following a Rolling Stones gig last year, which has gone some way to inspiring this one).

Don't be afraid of old material. In January I presented to a team and knew perfectly well one or two of them had attended my standard media training presentation before. I was rather concerned that they'd spot the same stories coming up; in fact, when one of them nipped to the loo, she came back and asked whether I'd got to the bit about the software operating system yet - she had re-hired me because she wanted her colleagues to hear the same stories, not to avoid them.

Likewise the Stranglers were performing new material but also slotted in a hell of a lot of the stuff from the seventies and early eighties - it wouldn't have been right without *Golden Brown*.

Don't be obsessive though - embrace change. Where it's right, change can be refreshing. Yes, a lot of people in the audience would have liked to have seen Hugh Cornwell back as lead singer but there's too much antagonism, it's not going to happen so Baz Warne is now on vocals - but rather than tuck him in the back and not draw attention to him, the band has embraced him as a full-blown front man, doing most of the announcements, joking with the audience - and he makes a damned good job of it.

The perfect example was when original drummer, Jet Black, came on two thirds of the way through - his health no longer allows him to play a full gig at 74. The stand-in was terrific, Black got a huge cheer when he came on and both played in the last number. Having two drummers should have looked clunky but because it was handled well it appeared seamless.

Get the lighting and other technology right. Support group The Godfathers were fine, but when the Stranglers came on the light show was great, it was all spectacular People were rushing in and out with the different guitars they needed, sound levels perfect. I once saw another noted performer of the same vintage at Crystal Palace and he was all but inaudible, even commenting on it to the audience. I wasn't there before either gig but I can guess which act put the hours in making sure everything would run smoothly before they came on - and it worked.

In terms of professional presentations and by the same token, I've seen speakers freeze because their video isn't working, cringe because their presentation has changed its font whilst on a memory stick - and I've also seen speakers who've done the technical run-through and made damned sure the audience doesn't pay for any IT glitch.

Give everybody basic respect. Yes the Stranglers were among the original, very edgy punks, but maybe because it was the last gig of the tour, Warne made sure he thanked a lot of people publicly including the sound, lighting, technical people by name - even the guys selling the merchandise at the back of the hall got a namecheck. The stage persona may be a bit snarly; nobody left the room in any doubt that the group appreciated everyone's work no matter what their role was.

Don't tell the Stranglers you're using them as examples of business advice. They are still slightly scary.

Oh, and be brilliant, leave the audience utterly gobsmacked, is always a good idea.

Embrace the elephant in the room

This bandage thing is coming in more useful than I thought. For anyone not following me on Facebook, LinkedIn etc. I'm currently swathed in a head bandage. The current model is brown rather than the pristine white in this pic but you get the idea. Basically I had a few hereditary and harmless cysts removed and the bandage is a precaution to ensure infection doesn't set in.

It went on last Wednesday and if I'm honest I wasn't looking forward to the two speaking engagements I had on Friday and Saturday, particularly given its tendency to pop off (which it did, in mid-presentation on Friday, to the merriment of the audience. I was just thinking of the hygiene issue of putting a bandage back on after it had been on the floor).

What I've found is that people don't mind, and if you carry on regardless you get a reputation as a bit of a trouper when you don't let it stop you working.

Tips

Here are a few hints, then, if you ever find yourself presenting with something so glaringly visual and likely to distract the audience:

- Don't try to ignore something if it's this big.

- Take ownership - once I'd decided I wasn't going to duck out of any duties, I made sure the pic was on Facebook, Twitter, LinkedIn, everywhere - don't give anyone else the opportunity to take charge!

- Get in first with the jokes - I introduced myself as Papa Smurf, said I might look bad but you should see the Andrex puppy, all that stuff. The audience will relax because you're laughing with them.

- When a tactless oaf comes up for a bit of networking and suggests you remove the bandage as you're off stage now, and refuses to believe it's genuine, refrain from punching them in the face. No, I didn't actually hit the guy, I resisted - but if he thinks I'm returning his emails he has another thing coming.

> **"If something is going to distract an audience, turn it into an asset."**

Paying for speakers

I was frustrated yesterday to find myself negotiating for a speaking deal that is now unlikely to happen. I get the feeling I should have trusted my instincts and walked away sooner - and would like to share some reasoning, hopefully this will be useful to other event organisers. Mostly it came down to money. My agent at Jillie Bushell Associates said the client pretty much thought I should be speaking for the pleasure of it.

If there were only one statement to take away from this blog entry then it is that speakers do mostly enjoy what they do for a living and we realise this is a privilege for which we've worked, not some sort of right. However, if an event organiser is in their office being paid for their time and calling us to value our own time at zero, then it's not a great start.

They came back to me with a price much lower than I'd normally work for. I suggested a few things we could do to make it work; find a sponsor to add extra cash, in exchange for which I would mention the sponsor in one minute out of about 40 (so definitely no hard sell); they could give me the list of attendees so I could market seminars to them afterwards, they could make a high-res video of the presentation for me to use in future marketing materials, they could buy one of my books for everyone and of course I'd take a cut from that. They were OK with the book proposal but tried to talk me down on price; I pointed out that since the idea of this was to compensate for a very low fee, there wasn't a deal to be done. That's where we are at the moment.

Thoughts

There are a few lessons to take away from this:

- **Speakers**, as well as facilitators and anyone else being approached for their time, trust your instincts. If someone comes in expecting you to work for free then there may well be no deal to be done. You could save time by walking away, politely, sooner rather than later.

- **Organisers**, have some basic respect - you're asking us to add value to your conference, there needs to be value to us as well. And if we come back with other ideas as to how this might work, at least understand that we're trying to make this work for you (and us) - a dismissive attitude does you no favours. Again, backing out politely sooner rather than later if you know there's no movement available to you could well save you a lot of time.

- **Both sides**, if there's an agency involved respect what they're doing as well. It would be unethical of me to offer people who've spoken to my agent a better deal, why would I undercut the person who's working on my behalf? Coming to me separately after speaking to my representative and seeing if you can get a better price is something I might classify as 'sneaky' - if a deal does emerge from all this, the client will no doubt be stunned when I tell them my agent is involved and will be taking her cut; the fact is, she started the negotiation off. I don't expect her to work for nothing. Anyone overtly asks me if there's a better deal going without my agent being involved, I back out.

- **Organisers** - if you get someone to work for nothing, and you might, ask yourself why they're doing it. You may get a compromised speech. If it's for a cause in which they believe, fine - if the British Heart Foundation wants me to speak for them and waive the fee anytime I'm up for it. If the speaker is trying ideas out, they might waive the fee but organisers should be aware this won't be a completed presentation, it's a work in progress. They may just be new speakers looking for experience, and if an organiser doesn't mind trying someone out for the first time that's

> OK. It's more likely that a 'free' speaker will use your stage time to sell their own services - why else would they get up on their hind legs and perform for nothing? - and this hits the organiser's reputation.

Finally if you're among the clients who expect us to do something for nothing, please be aware that we're going to wheedle some value out of it somehow. Giving us a decent fee enables us to focus entirely on your needs rather than our own - isn't that a better deal?

How to handle/not handle a freelance

OK, yesterday I had a meeting with a new prospect. I may or may not be doing some work with the company; it doesn't matter (well, financially it does) but the way he approached the meeting was exemplary and worth sharing - this attitude is certain to bring out better results for both sides, so a number of elements are worth sharing.

Flexibility: He had an objective in mind and an idea of how I could help. However, he was secure enough to admit that his own strategy might not be the right one to take him to the point he wanted to get to so he was interested to hear my ideas (in my view he was spot on in the first place). He genuinely wanted to listen rather than tell me what service he wanted - this gave me freedom to tailor my thoughts according to his needs.

Objective: A subset of that first point is that he had an objective. Loads of people want to talk to journalists, to get some copy put together for their website or whatever they want, but they haven't thought through to an end game - so they can't measure whether their project has actually worked.

Openness: Straight off, he told me a bit about the budget he'd been given and what he wanted to get out of it. This isn't always necessary but his transparency helped, and encouraged me, in the same spirit, to be completely open about the elements with which I couldn't help.

Research: I'm under no illusions, when I'm pitching to someone for corporate work it's down to me to do the research and find out about them, not the other way around. However, the fact that he'd found out a little about what I do, taken a glance at the website to make sure his impressions were current and soforth, helped us to get to the common ground very quickly.

Location: This guy is based miles from me. Once again, I'm pitching, it is absolutely incumbent on me to make his life easier rather than the other way round. However, he knew he was going to be close by so he suggested we make it mutually convenient. Compare and contrast this with the guy who once asked me down to his office in Guildford, failed completely to offer me any coffee and then asked me for information I'd already sent him - guess who I'd rather be working with.

Avoiding hesitation

Something a number of media presenters ask me when I'm training is how they can avoid hesitation, umm-ing and aah-ing, repetition and all those other things that would lose you a round in "Just a Minute". They also want tips on how to remember their stuff without notes, they've seen *Dragons' Den*.

The answer is simple. You're not doing those shows so their rules don't apply. So often I find people get really hung up on this stuff. So here are a few tips:

- Take notes into an interview with you as long as they're not going to be in shot on TV. Nobody is going to be offended by the fact that you've taken some time to prepare.

- Listen to everyday conversations. People stumble over sentences, they start and stop again, they repeat themselves. The listener filters out one heck of a lot and will do the same for you. There are people who adopt the glossy, completely slick approach; if that's not you, don't sweat about it. Be natural when presenting to any audience and they'll forgive more or less anything.

- Prepare and get your message out there as quickly as you can - people's attention spans are shrinking in the Internet age so the sooner you make your immediate impact the better.

- Unless you have a particular issue with body language, don't sweat about finessing it too much. People always look much worse when they're self-consciously trying to avoid doing something than when they're just speaking fluently. Obviously if you become aware of a particular habit it can be good to get it under control.

- Try to have a 'critical friend' present and don't take their criticism personally. I did a stand-up gig last night which went OK; feedback from fellow (and much more experienced) comedian Paul Warricker was invaluable.

Look for the light - my colleague at the Professional Speaking Association, Celia Delaney, made this point at our Spring Convention earlier this year. Many excellent speakers get up onto a stage and then look down at the audience, which is fine but it can leave your face in shadows. Use your eyes to look at the audience but make sure they can see your face.

Engage with the press

So last week I'm at a press event - which one isn't important, loads of gadgets on display from multiple vendors. The idea is that they want us (the press and blogger community) to write about this stuff.

So I did a little experiment. I walked up and down the aisles, slowly, smiling benignly at the people manning the stands.

A lot clearly had not been briefed about how to handle the press. Or even that they should be doing so. I wasn't there to be difficult, I promise, but on the whole if you have someone walking past you with 'freelance journalist' on your badge at a press event, slowly, making eye contact, it's not a problem to ask them who they write for, can you interest them in your products and soforth.

Drifting past

There were three aisles of exhibitors and I managed to do a pass-through of one of them without (I am not exaggerating) anyone attempting to talk to me.

Of course I went back and took the initiative, and you can expect to see a number of the things I saw coming up on my LifeOver35 blog.

But if you happened to be in PR, and you had clients about to exhibit at a show in which journalists would be attending or which - as in last week's example - is dedicated to journalists investigating technology or whatever the show is dedicated to, do give them a briefing on talking to us - it's why we're there.

I have this disturbing image of Lord Sugar in the boardroom, incredulously asking the exhibitors 'You had a journalist working for the Guardian and the Times, actually slowing down and smiling at you, and you ignored him?' I bet I wasn't the only one.

Conclusion

TAX
wages
RATE RISE
business
tax
Shares dive despite profit boost
tax pl
profits
funding
Mighty
trade
tax pl

That's kind of it so far. Like any blog there can be and will be more – do have a look at clapperton.co.uk often and see what I've added, who's done what either well or dreadfully and there should hopefully be loads more to say. But if you take anything away from this book then let's make it:

- You don't work for us
- We don't work for you
- You need to prepare for interviews and presentations
- Working with audiences is always going to be a help, whether in your usual field or not
- Use the bridging technique to get back to your comfort zone
- Don't speak about stuff for which you haven't prepared or which is not in your area

Above all try to have fun with it. Yes there are a couple of aggressive journalists out there who think they're going to be the next Jeremy Paxman and for all we know one or two of them might be right. The majority, though, are going to be after a straightforward interview to get facts right.

Good luck!

About the author

Guy Clapperton, a Fellow of the Professional Speaking Association, is the author of "This Is Social Media," "This Is Social Commerce", "Free Publicity for your Business in a Week" and co-author of "The Joy of Work?" alongside Prof. Peter Warr. A business/technology journalist and broadcaster since 1989, he has seen the impact both positive and negative of the Internet and universal communications first hand.

Guy can add value to your event by speaking on any of his three core topics:

Talk to the press

Media engagement can be brilliant for business or completely disastrous. Guy, a media trainer since 2002, may not have seen it all but he's seen a fair bit and can entertain and inform on how things can go well or badly, and offer some practical insights into pitfalls and interview techniques.

Social Media

As the author of two books on the subject Guy can speak about examples where business has been transformed by social media – and damned nearly killed by it. Guy will offer a lively insight into just what can go right and wrong, Did you hear the one about the high-profile fashion designer who tried to hijack the riots in Cairo to promote his sale..?

Unified communications, the next generation

Suppose you could hold your phone up to the street and have it tell you which shops offered WiFi and then tell you what other people thought of the signal and ambiance? Guy has been able to do this for years as has anyone else with the right app – so is business ready for the next generation of workers? In his 'business futurologist' mode, Guy looks at the expectations of an incoming generation that takes bringing its own iPad into work as read, which doesn't understand why anyone would want to use a land line and which has grown up with Facebook as a mainstream environment. Guy looks at this generation both as customers and employees.

Guy has been a speaker since the middle of the last decade and in 2012 became a Fellow of the Professional Speaking Association. He has spoken on media and social media in 11 countries since 2011, broadcasts occasionally on the BBC News Channel and is spending his mid-life crisis attempting a few stand-up spots in London comedy clubs.

He will welcome the chance to talk through your needs and to find how he can add value to your event – check his website at:

www.clapperton.co.uk

or mail Guy@Clapperton.co.uk.

"Journalism largely consists in saying 'Lord Jones Dead' to people who never knew Lord Jones was alive."

– G. K. Chesterton.

Notes

Notes

Notes

Notes

www.ingramcontent.com/pod-product-compliance
Lightning Source LLC
LaVergne TN
LVHW010102110826
845155LV00028B/448
* 9 7 8 1 9 0 8 6 9 3 1 2 9 *